Killer Snakes

Cottonmouth

By Karlie Gambino

Gareth Stevens Publishing

Please visit our website, www.garethstevens.com. For a free color catalog of all our high-quality books, call toll free 1-800-542-2595 or fax 1-877-542-2596.

Library of Congress Cataloging-in-Publication Data

Gambino, Karlie.
Cottonmouth / Karlie Gambino.
p. cm. — (Killer snakes)
Includes index.
ISBN 978-1-4339-5640-9 (pbk.)
ISBN 978-1-4339-5641-6 (6-pack)
ISBN 978-1-4339-5638-6 (library binding)
1. Agkistrodon piscivorus—Juvenile literature. I. Title.
QL666.O69G36 2011
597.96'3—dc22

2010048668

First Edition

Published in 2012 by
Gareth Stevens Publishing
111 East 14th Street, Suite 349
New York, NY 10003

Designer: Michael J. Flynn
Editor: Greg Roza

Photo credits: Cover, pp. 1, (pp. 2–4, 6, 8, 10, 12, 14, 16, 18, 20–24 snake skin texture), 5, 11, 13 (all), 14–15, 17, 19, 21 Shutterstock.com; p. 7 Joel Sartore/National Geographic/Getty Images; p. 9 Gerold & Cynthia Merker/Visuals Unlimited/Getty Images.

Printed in the United States of America

CPSIA compliance information: Batch #CS11GS: For further information contact Gareth Stevens, New York, New York at 1-800-542-2595.

Contents

Boldface words appear in the glossary.

Open Up, Cottonmouth!

The cottonmouth is the only **venomous** water snake in North America. It lives in the southeastern United States. When a cottonmouth is in danger, it **coils** up and hisses. This shows the cotton-white color inside its mouth.

KEY
cottonmouth

Daily Life

Cottonmouths live around slow streams, lakes, ponds, and **marshes**. During the day, they lie in the sun. This warms them as they rest. At night, they hunt. Piles of leaves and fallen trees make good hiding spots.

Blending In

A cottonmouth's coloring helps it blend in with its surroundings. Cottonmouths can be tan, brown, black, or dark green. Most have bands of brown and black. Often, the cottonmouth's **prey** doesn't see the snake hiding until it's too late!

Cottonmouth Bodies

Adult cottonmouths are about 24 to 48 inches (61 to 122 cm) long. They weigh about 2 to 4 pounds (0.9 to 1.8 kg). Males are commonly larger than females. Cottonmouths have thick bodies and thin tails. Their heads are wide and flat.

Growing Up

Female cottonmouths commonly have 10 to 16 babies once every other year. Babies have yellow tails they use to **lure** prey. As a cottonmouth ages, its color darkens and its bands fade. Older cottonmouths are often a single dark color.

baby
adult

Cottonmouth Venom

A cottonmouth uses its venom to catch prey. When a cottonmouth bites, its two **fangs** shoot venom into its prey. Cottonmouth venom is very strong. It causes the animal to bleed to death.

Deadly Hunter

Sometimes cottonmouths chase prey. Other times they hide and **attack** when prey comes by. Cottonmouths eat frogs, lizards, snakes, turtles, baby alligators, mice, birds, and fish. They even eat smaller cottonmouths.

Cottonmouths have heat-sensing spots on their faces called pits. The pits help them find prey in the dark. Their mouths snap shut like traps! Cottonmouths hold on to their prey until the venom starts working. Once their prey dies, cottonmouths swallow the meal whole!

Cottonmouths and People

Cottonmouths may attack people when they are surprised or hurt. Their venom causes pain, swelling, and heavy bleeding. Their bites don't often cause death, but they can. Someone who is bitten needs a special drug called antivenin.

Glossary

attack: to try to hurt someone or something

coil: to curl around and around

fang: a long, sharp tooth

lure: to trick an animal into coming closer

marsh: an area with wet ground and long grass

prey: an animal that is hunted by others for food

venomous: containing venom, which is a harmful liquid

For More Information

Books

Doeden, Matt. *Cottonmouths.* Mankato, MN: Capstone Press, 2005.

Sexton, Colleen. *Cottonmouths.* Minneapolis, MN: Bellwether Media, 2010.

Websites

***Agkistrodon piscivorus* (cottonmouth)**
animaldiversity.ummz.umich.edu/site/accounts/information/Agkistrodon_piscivorus.html
Read about cottonmouths and see pictures of them.

Cottonmouth
nationalzoo.si.edu/Animals/ReptilesAmphibians/Facts/FactSheets/Cottonmouth.cfm
Read more about cottonmouth snakes.

Index